Bajan
Cooking

Sally Miller

acknowledgements

Created and written by: Sally Miller
Photography: Artie
Food styling: Sally Miller
Layout: Ashif Nakhuda
Illustrations and Design: Neil Barnard

Published by: Miller Publishing Co. Ltd.,
Williams Industrial Park,
Edgehill,
St. Thomas, BARBADOS
Telephone: (246) 421-6700
Fax: (246) 421-6707
e-mail: sally@millerpublishing.net

ISBN 978-976-95153-7-6

Printed in Singapore

contents

foreword

This is a selection of Bajan recipes from my Contemporary Caribbean Cookbook. The methods have been written very precisely with full explanations that are easy for anyone to follow. A great deal of testing has been carried out to ensure that the recipes really work.

People in the Caribbean will rejoice in a cookbook featuring ingredients that are readily available throughout the region, but this cookbook is not intended to be limited to the sole use of people resident in the islands. On the contrary, West Indians living abroad and all friends of the Caribbean should also be able to make these dishes, wherever in the world they live, since the vast majority of the ingredients required can now be purchased in most major supermarkets.

I hope that my recipes will inspire people to get into the kitchen and prepare a wonderful variety of good Bajan food regularly. Preparing good food for yourself and your family everyday is surely the best ticket to health and happiness. It really is quite easy to do!

Happy Cooking!

Sally

measurements & equipment

Measurements

Measuring with cups and spoons is an easy way to cook and this is the first measurement given in each recipe. For those who are in the habit of cooking with scales and measuring jugs, each ingredient is also given in metric and imperial amounts. For those willing to convert to the cup system, get yourself two sets of the measuring cups shown here. It's useful to have a set for wet and then dry ingredients.

Equipment

I have tried to make cooking easy and quick. This book is different in that equipment is brought into play to make cooking simpler and easier. A lightweight food processor and a hand blender are a boon to any cook. A lightweight food processor that can be lifted in and out of the cupboard with one hand means that it is easy to use. All you need on a daily basis is the steel blade and bowl. The other attachments won't be needed very often. Rather than write a cookbook with more of the same cake recipes, I have written them using a food processor. This makes the cake as easy to make as the instant box variety.

Speed is what today's busy cooks need.

bajan seasoning

This is a cornerstone of tasty Bajan cooking. This wonderful timesaver is used to season fish, chicken, meats, dips, stocks and soups. It is available ready made, however, the homemade version in this recipe is especially delicious and it keeps for months in the fridge.

6oz/185g green topped spring onions
1 head of garlic
1lb/500g (6–7 medium) Spanish onions
4 sprigs of fresh thyme
4 sprigs of fresh marjoram
Handful of fresh parsley
Handful of fresh basil
1 tablespoon curry
1 tablespoon salt
1 tablespoon celery salt
1 tablespoon paprika

2 tablespoons fresh ground black pepper
1/2 teaspoon ground cloves
1 very hot red pepper or 3 chili peppers
or 2 tablespoons of red pepper sauce

Optional:
Handful of fresh coriander
(cilantro, chardon beni)
Handful of celery leaves
All purpose powdered seasonings
Cumin and turmeric

1. Chop up the spring onions.
2. Peel and chop the Spanish onions.
3. Peel all the garlic.
4. Pick the leaves off the stems of the thyme, marjoram and parsley.
5. Place all the ingredients into a food processor and process for about 5 minutes.
6. Store in the fridge in two 10oz/300ml or one 20oz/600ml glass jar.

Barbados pepper sauce

Bajan pepper sauces, sparingly used, add the taste of Barbados to almost anything. Pepper lovers just can't get enough of the stuff. In the 1950's fresh horseradish was widely grown in Barbados and was a main ingredient in Bajan yellow pepper sauce. However, as the sauce became a commercial product, this wonderful ingredient faded out. This is an original old Bajan recipe. A hunk of cheddar cheese, some crackers, and a little bowl of this yellow sauce make a perfect snack to serve with drinks.

4oz/125g green topped spring onions
4-5 medium onions
12 very hot fresh peppers (bonnet) or
24 chili peppers
1/2oz/15g fresh turmeric or 1 teaspoon
powdered turmeric
2 tablespoons English hot mustard

1/4 cup 1oz/30g salt
2 1/2 cups vinegar
6 cloves garlic
1lb/500g grated fresh horseradish root
or 1 tablespoon horseradish powder
(optional)
3 dozen peeled pearl onions (optional)

1. Wash, peel and coarsely chop the spring onion and onions. Remove the stems from the peppers and for a less hot pepper sauce, remove the seeds. Peel the garlic.
2. Place the onions, turmeric, mustard, salt, peppers, garlic and 1/2 cup vinegar in a food processor and process for a few minutes. When processing be careful to wrap a kitchen towel around the lid as some processors spew when a thin liquid is processed.
3. Add 2 cups vinegar, the grated horseradish and whole pearl onions. (optional)
4. Store in clean bottles.

drinks

Rum Punch

1 measure of lime juice, freshly squeezed
2 measures of sugar syrup (no. 1)
3 measures of dark Caribbean rum,
the older, the better
4 measures of water or passion fruit juice
Dash of Angostura Bitters and freshly
grated nutmeg

1. Place two measures of sugar in a
   saucepan with a little water and cook
   until the sugar has dissolved and add to
   the juice.
2. Add the rum and water. A good quality
   passion fruit juice can be used instead of
   water but reduce the syrup slightly.
3. Serve with plenty of ice, a dash of bitters
   and a grating of nutmeg.

Banana Daiquiri

1 banana
1 measure of Caribbean rum
1 cup 8floz/250ml chipped ice
1 tablespoon lime juice
2 tablespoons light brown sugar

Place all the ingredients in a blender.
Blend for about 3 minutes.

Sangaree

1/2 cup 4floz/125ml Madeira
1 cup 8floz/250ml water
1 tablespoon freshly squeezed lime juice
light brown sugar syrup to taste
Nutmeg

Blend Madeira, water and lime juice. Sweeten
to taste. Pour over ice and serve with nutmeg.
A traditional 18th century mid-morning drink.
Barbados gave Queen Elizabeth ll a wedding
present of an antique Barbadian Sangaree jug

Bentley (Non Alcoholic)

1 measure of lime juice
1 measure of sugar syrup
Ice and water to fill 10oz/300ml tumbler
1 marashino cherry
Dash of Angostura bitters

Mix the lime, syrup, water and ice.
Top with a dash of bitters and a cherry.

Passiontini

1 measure vodka
1 /2 measure of passionfruit syrup
crushed ice

Mix well, Pour into a martini glass and
garnish with a few fresh passion fruit seeds.

salt fish cakes

This first fish cake recipe is the flour-based version served at elegant cocktail parties and rustic rum shops throughout Barbados, the latter being three or four times the size of the former. As health conscious as we are all trying to be, hot fish cakes passed around at a gathering go like smoke in the wind. They are also popular as a take-away item, with the tell-tale grease stains seeping through the little brown paper bags they are often sold in.

1/2lb/250g boneless salt fish
1 small onion finely chopped
3 cloves garlic finely chopped
1 tablespoon pepper sauce (optional)
1 1/4 cups 6oz/185g flour
2 teaspoons baking powder
1 egg
1/2 cup 4floz/125ml milk

1/2 cup 4floz/125ml water
1oz/30g butter
1/4 cup/2-3 finely chopped spring onions
Sprigs of thyme, parsley, marjoram picked off the stems and finely chopped
Freshly ground black pepper, white pepper and salt to taste

1. Place the salt fish in a saucepan with 6 cups of water. Bring to the boil for a few minutes, pour off the first set of water and bring it to the boil a second time in a fresh 4 cups of water for 1/2 hour. Check the saltiness of the fish. It should be salty but not overly so. If it is you may need to boil it up a third time.
2. Shred the salt fish with your fingers or a fork.
3. Put all of the ingredients in a mixing bowl and stir vigorously until a thick batter is formed.
4. Deep fry teaspoonfuls over a medium heat, until golden brown. Avoid the outside of the fish cakes burning before the middle is well cooked by carefully monitoring the heat.
5. Drain on absorbent kitchen paper.
6. Serve hot with Marie Rose Sauce or yellow Bajan pepper sauce (page 8).

pumpkin soup

The two main varieties of pumpkin found in Barbados are Garden and Belly. Belly pumpkin is more fibrous and most commonly used for soups. This soup is also delicious made with butternut squash.

1lb/500g chicken with bones and skin or
left over baked chicken bones
5 cups 40floz/1.2l of water
Sprigs of thyme, parsley and marjoram
Celery leaves or a stick of celery
1–2 whole, green topped spring onions
2 dark green outer cabbage leaves

1 tablespoon black peppercorns
1 onion
1 chicken stock cube
1oz/30g butter
3lbs/1.5kg pumpkin

Garnish: Fresh cream, parsley or thyme

1. If using chicken, remove any fat, but not the skin since it gives the stock a good flavour.
2. Place all the ingredients, except the pumpkin and the butter, into a saucepan. Bring to the boil and then simmer on a medium heat for 1/2 hour.
3. Remove the chicken, skin and bones from the stock by pouring it through a colander or strainer and return it to the heat. Add the pumpkin peeled and roughly chopped and the butter. Boil for 1/2 hour or until the pumpkin is well cooked. If using the chicken, either add the cooked chicken meat to the soup or use it otherwise.
4. Cool and mix in a blender and add salt and pepper to taste.
5. Freeze if not serving immediately.
6. When ready to serve, reheat over a medium heat.
7. Serve garnished with fresh parsley or a small blob of cream, dropped in the centre of each bowl and swirled gently with a pointed knife or toothpick.

Serves 4-6

plantains wrapped in bacon

Plantains are grown and eaten in Barbados. Masquerading themselves as very large bananas, these vegetables are unpalatable unless cooked, and can be prepared at all stages of ripeness, with stark contrasts of texture and flavour. When they are unripe, and as hard as potatoes, they may be peeled and boiled as a bland, starchy accompaniment to stews. Ripe, they can be baked whole in a medium oven for 15-20 minutes and served either in their skins or peeled and sliced. But it is when plantains are over-ripe and speckled with black that they are best sliced diagonally and sautéed in a little shallow oil. It possesses a deniable but subtle sweetness that goes exceptionally well with chicken, pork, and fish.

3 ripe plantains   6oz/185g pack of streaky bacon

1. Preheat the oven to 350F 180C or Gas Mark 4.
2. Cut the pack of streaky bacon down the centre.
3. Peel the plantains and cut them into pieces of 2"/5cm in length.
4. Wrap each piece of plantain in 1/2 a piece of streaky bacon.
5. Bake the plantains for 20-25 mins or until a nice colour brown.

Serves 6-8

plantain rissoles

4 ripe or yellow plantains   Salt and pepper
1 tsp butter   Oil for frying

Use plantains that are not ripe enough to slice or fry.
1. Boil plantains in salted water until tender. Drain and mash until smooth.
2. Allow to cool then add the butter. Form into rissoles and fry.

pumpkin fritters

The creamier Garden Pumpkin is most commonly served boiled or in fritters while the slightly more fibrous Belly pumpkin is more suited to soups. Pumpkin fritters are served sprinkled with sugar and spice, but they are eaten as a side dish, not a dessert.

2lbs/1kg pumpkin
Salt
3 tablespoons brown sugar
2 teaspoons mixed powdered spice or cinnamon
1 egg
1 cup 5oz/155g flour

2 tablespoons milk
2 teaspoons baking powder
Canola oil for frying
Garnish: 2 tablespoons brown sugar mixed with 1 teaspoon mixed powdered spice

1. Peel, cut up and boil the pumpkin in salted water until soft.
2. Drain pumpkin very thoroughly to avoid watery fritters and mash. In a little bowl mix the sugar and spice and add to the pumpkin.
3. Whisk an egg and mix into the pumpkin along with the milk. Add baking powder and flour until it comes to a good dropping consistency.
4. Shallow fry both sides on a medium heat until dark brown. Adjust heat when cooking so fritters cook through without burning. These fritters should be fairly thin with a creamy consistency inside when cooked.
5. Serve hot, sprinkled with the mixture of sugar and spice.

Makes 20-25 fritters.

dressed cucumber and tomato

Cucumber, lime and salt creates a wonderful "ménage à trois". This salad is delicious served as a side dish with fish or fish cakes.

This tomato salad makes tomatoes come alive. They spring their own juices and the left over juices can be bottled and used as a dressing at a later date.

Dressed Cucumber

1lb/500g cucumbers
1 teaspoon salt
1 tablespoon lime juice
1/2 tablespoon onion finely chopped
1/2 tablespoon white vinegar
1/2 teaspoon red hot pepper very finely chopped (optional).

1. Peel the cucumbers, leaving on some slivers of skin for colour and nutrition. Slice thinly.
2. Place in a bowl with salt, lime juice, onion, vinegar and hot pepper if using. Mix well and allow to stand for about 1/2 hour before serving.

Bajan Tomato Salad

1lb/500g full ripe tomatoes
1 medium red onion thinly sliced (optional)
Salt and freshly ground black pepper
2 sprigs of fresh thyme
1/4 cup 4floz/125ml olive oil
2 tablespoons salad vinegar

1. Wash and thickly slice tomatoes. Place on the serving dish along with the sliced onions if including.
2. Sprinkle with salt and pepper.
3. Sprinkle on the thyme leaves.
4. Pour over the olive oil and vinegar.
5. Serve immediately or refrigerate for up to 2 hours.

steamed rice

Not all plain steamed rice is created equal - subtle seasoning and thorough washing makes the world of difference.

4 cups 32floz/960ml water
3/4 teaspoon salt
1/2 chicken stock cube
1 tablespoon butter
1 small onion finely chopped
1 1/2 cups 12floz/360ml rice

1. Put the water, salt, stock cube, butter and onion in a medium saucepan and bring to the boil.
2. Wash the rice thoroughly in a bowl of water, strain, repeat and add to water.
3. Boil uncovered on medium heat for 10 minutes.
4. Cover tightly and reduce heat to low. Let it steam until all the water is absorbed (15-20 minutes).

split peas & rice

4 cups 32floz/960ml water
3/4 teaspoon salt
2 cups chicken stock
2 tablespoons butter
1 small onion finely chopped
1 1/2 cups 12floz/360ml rice
1 salted pig tail, washed
1 cup yellow split peas
Large sprig of fresh thyme

1. Wash the rice and peas thoroughly in a bowl of water, strain and repeat.
2. Put the water, chicken stock, rice, split peas, salt, butter, thyme, pig tail and onion in a medium saucepan and bring to the boil until peas are tender.
3. Boil uncovered on medium heat for 10 minutes.
4. Cover tightly and reduce heat to low. Let it steam until all the water is absorbed and rice and peas are tender (15-20 minutes). Add more hot water if necessary.

pigeon peas & rice

Peas and rice is a dish that is eaten throughout the Caribbean. Pigeon peas are related to the tender green sweet peas but are much higher in protein and vitamins, making this a very nutritious dish.

2 cups 11oz/345g fresh/frozen pigeon peas or 1 cup of dried pigeon peas
6 cups 48floz/1.45l water
Bouquet garni of fresh thyme, marjoram and chives
1/4lb/125g salt beef or salt pork

1 tablespoon butter
2 cups 8floz/250ml rice
1 large tomato, blanched, peeled and chopped up
1 tablespoon lime juice
Red pepper sauce to taste

Using Fresh/Frozen Pigeon Peas

1. Cover and boil the peas, herbs and salt beef in four cups of water for about 1/2 hour. If you are not using salt meat, add salt to taste.
2. Wash the rice and drain. Add the rice, 2 more cups of water, butter, tomato and lime juice.
3. Bring to the boil, cover and cook on medium heat for 5 minutes.
4. Reduce heat to low and let it simmer until all the water is steamed out (20-25 minutes).

Using Dried Pigeon Peas

1. If using dried pigeon peas increase the water to 7 cups and cook the dried peas very rapidly for about 10-15 minutes and then reduce to simmer for about 40 minutes or until tender.
2. Proceed with the recipe (left) at 2.

breadfruit in butter sauce

Captain William Bligh was chosen to lead an expedition to the South Seas to bring the breadfruit to the Caribbean. On his first attempt, his devotion to the breadfruit saplings and neglect of his crew's water needs lead to the famous mutiny on the Bounty. Cast overboard, Captain Bligh made his way hundreds of miles to safety in an open boat. On his second attempt in 1793 he sailed into Jamaica's Port Royal Harbour with a ship so crowded with beautiful leafy breadfruit saplings that the Jamaicans rowed out toward "the ship that have bush". Today large, lush breadfruit trees grow throughout Barbados bearing the football like starchy staple that has kept hunger away from many a door.

1/2 medium breadfruit
1/2 small onion
1 tablespoon olive oil
4oz/125g butter
1-2 medium onions, cut in rings
1 tablespoon garlic finely chopped
1 tablespoon lime juice

1 medium 16floz/500ml tin whole
tomatoes, drained and sliced
1/4 cup/3 tablespoons parsley, diced
Salt and pepper to taste
1 cup 8oz/250ml water
Red pepper sauce to taste
Garnish: fresh parsley, chopped

1. Cut the breadfruit, remove the seeds in the core and peel. Boil in salted water with a little onion and oil, over a high heat until tender and drain.
2. Meanwhile, melt the butter in a frying pan and lightly brown the onion rings. Add the garlic, tomatoes, parsley, lime juice, salt and pepper. Continue to sauté for a couple of minutes. Add the water, bring to the boil and simmer for 5-10 minutes.
3. Slice the cooled breadfruit and place in a serving dish. Pour the butter sauce over the breadfruit.
4. Garnish with chopped fresh parsley.

Serves 4

pickled breadfruit

Often served with souse, pickled breadfruit is also a delicious side dish served with fish or roast pork. It can be made well ahead of serving and kept in the fridge. It is a very healthy dish.

1/2 medium breadfruit
1 tablespoon oil
Pickle:
1lb/500g small cucumber, peeled, deseeded and very finely chopped
1/4 cup 1 small onion finely chopped
Salt to taste

1/3 cup parsley finely chopped
Fresh hot pepper very finely chopped to taste (about 1/4 deseeded pepper)
1 medium sweet pepper finely chopped
3-6 tablespoons lime juice, to taste
Garnish: fresh parsley, sweet pepper

1. Cut the breadfruit, remove the seeds in the core and peel. Boil in salted water and oil, over a high heat until just tender. Drain and cool.
2. Meanwhile, prepare the pickle ingredients and mix well. Remove any seeds from the cucumber. Put enough salt and lime juice to make a nice, acid, salty pickle since the bland breadfruit quickly counteracts it.
3. Slice the breadfruit, mix into the pickle. Place in a serving dish and garnish with parsley and sweet pepper rings.

Serves 4-6

breadfruit chips

1 parboiled breadfruit   Cooking oil

1. Place parboiled breadfruit in the fridge overnight. Next day, slice it as thinly as possible and fry in deep oil using a chip basket.
2. Sprinkle salt over them while they are still hot.

breadfruit cou cou

1 breadfruit
2 cups 16floz/500ml chicken stock
1/4 lb/125g salt meat
2 tbsp butter

1 bunch fresh herbs
2 tsp salt
1 chipped onion

1. Peel and cut the breadfruit into slices, removing the spongy centre. Boil with salt meat cut in pieces, herbs, onion and water.
2. When soft take from heat and crush with potato masher, then with a heavy wooden spoon to make smooth. Add stock as necessary. Stir in some of the butter and when smooth place in a dish and spread with the remainder of the butter.

roast breadfruit

1 breadfruit, full but not ripe
1/2lb/250g beef or pork
1 thick slice ham or 1/4 salt beef or pork

1 tomato
1 small onion
2-3 blades of spring onion leaves
1 tbsp butter

1. Peel and parboil breadfruit whole in salted water. Finely chop up meat and other ingredients and fry lightly in butter. Cool breadfruit and from the stalk end cut out core and a little fruit. Fill hole with prepared mixture.
2. Bake in a moderate oven till soft and brown - about 45 minutes.
Butter crust and serve hot.

macaroni cheese

Referred to in Barbados simply as "pie", macaroni cheese, served daily all across the island, is always a winner, especially with children. There are several variations to this dish. It can also be made with different kinds of pasta such as penne or rotini. Adding 2 tins of tuna is also an option to make a one pot meal served with salad.

8oz/250g macaroni
1 tablespoon butter or margarine
1 1/2 lbs/675g sharp cheddar cheese, grated
1 egg
1 cup 8floz/240ml evaporated milk
1 small grated onion
1 teaspoon hot English mustard
1 tablespoon yellow mustard
1 teaspoon white pepper

1 teaspoon salt
1/2 teaspoon red pepper sauce or cayenne pepper (optional)
1 1/2 tablespoons tomato ketchup
1 finely chopped sweet pepper (optional)
Garnish:
2 tablespoons fine breadcrumbs
2 teaspoons butter
2 tablespoons grated cheddar cheese

1. Bring water to the boil. Break up macaroni and add to the boiling water with salt. Boil it uncovered until it is just tender but not overcooked (about 8 minutes).
2. Preheat oven to 350F, 180C or Gas Mark 4.
3. Drain the macaroni thoroughly, put it back into the same hot saucepan it was cooked in and mix in the butter.
4. Grate the cheese and mix it in with the macaroni a bit at a time, while it is still warm.
5. Whisk the egg until fluffy and add the milk, onion powder, white pepper, salt, pepper sauce and mustard. Pour in with the macaroni and mix.
6. Place in a greased oven proof casserole dish. Top with a little butter, some grated cheese and fine breadcrumbs. Bake in the centre of the oven for about 30-45 minutes depending on the depth of the dish.

sweet potato or yam pie

Ground provisions play an important role in the diet of Barbadians and are often cited by Barbados' many centenarians as a reason for their longevity. Sweet potatoes and yams in particular are good sources of energy - they are slowly metabolised by the body and contain many vitamins and minerals. The great thing about ground provision pies is they can be made well ahead of time.

2 1/2 lbs/1.25kg sweet potatoes or yam
1 teaspoon salt
1 tablespoon oil
1 egg
4oz/125g butter

1 cup 8floz/250ml milk
Salt and pepper to taste

Garnish: Fine breadcrumbs, grated cheese and a tablespoon of butter

1. Peel and cut up the sweet potatoes or yams and put them into water immediately to avoid discolouring. Make sure that the saucepan has enough water to cover them, add the oil and a teaspoon of salt and bring to the boil. Simmer on a medium heat until soft, (about 20 minutes). Peel and thickly slice the yam, under running water. Place in a saucepan of salted water immediately to prevent discolouring. Wash hands and arms thoroughly as some yam skin causes itching.
2. Whisk the egg. Drain the sweet potatoes/yams and while they are still hot add the egg, butter, milk and salt and pepper to taste. Mash using a hand blender or potato masher.
3. Grease a casserole dish and fill with the mashed potato or yam mixture. You can add some extra grated cheese to a yam pie.
4. Sprinkle the top of the potato or yam with some fine breadcrumbs and a few dabs of butter. Bake in a moderate oven for 25 minutes.

Serves 4-6

easy corn pie

Here's a pie that's 'easy as pie', in fact it must be the easiest pie around.

1. Beat eggs and add the ingredients in the order of listing. Mix lightly. If you want a light "souffle" type of corn pie, separate the eggs, beat the egg whites until stiff and fold into the rest of the ingredients including the egg yolks.
2. Pour into buttered casserole dish. Bake at 180C, 350F Gas mark 3 until firm. (about 15 minutes.)

Serves 6-8

2 eggs
2 tablespoons milk
1-2 tablespoons brown sugar
1/2 teaspoon vanilla essence
1 can 15oz/425g cream style corn
1 can 15oz/425g whole kernel corn, drained
2 tablespoons butter (softened)
Dash of Angostura bitters (optional)

corn soup

This is a delicious vegetarian soup that is easy to make and popular.

1. Brown the onions in the butter.
2. Add the split peas and simmer until tender.
3. Chop the corn into four or five pieces and add everything else to the soup.
4. Simmer until corn is tender, making sure that the split peas don't catch by stirring often.

Serves 6-8

2 cups split peas
2 onions
2 tins cream style corn
6 ears of fresh or frozen corn
Bunch fresh coriander or chardon beni
Salt and pepper to taste
Bouquet garni of fresh herbs

conkies

2 cups 12oz/375g cornmeal
1/2 cup 3oz/100g flour
3/4 lb/375g pumpkin
6 oz/185g butter
1/2 lb/250g sweet potato
4 oz/125g raisin
3/4 lb/375g brown sugar
1 cup 8floz/250ml milk
1 tsp mixed spice
1/2 tsp grated nutmeg
1 tsp almond essence
1 tsp salt
Banana or plantain leaves, steamed
and cut in 8" squares

1. Grate coconut, pumpkin and sweet potato.
2. Mix in sugar, liquids and spices.
3. Add raisins and flour last and combine well.
4. Melt shortening before adding with milk etc.
5. Fold a few tablespoons of the mixture in a 8" peice of banana or plantain leaf. Fold edges over to make a neat parcel and tie securely with string.
6. Place conkies on a rack and steam in a large saucepan for one hour, cover plantain and banana leaves.

sorrel

1/4 lb/125g dried sorrel sepals
piece dried orange peel
cinnamon stick
few whole cloves
8 cups 1Gl/2L boiling water
2-3 lbs/500g-1.5kg light brown sugar
1 tsp powdered cinnamon
1/2 tsp powdered cloves
1/2 cup 125ml rum (optional)

1. Put the sorrel, dried orange peel, stick of cinnamon, and whole cloves in a earthen ware jar and pour the boiling water over.
2. When cool, cover and leave the mixture to steep for two days. Strain off the liquid, add sugar to taste, powdered spices and rum (optional) and allow it to stand another two days.
3. Serve chilled with plenty of ice.

pickled green bananas

Green bananas are another healthy starch alternative enjoyed by Barbadians. The bunches of thin, hard and bright green bananas are sold in markets and supermarkets year round. With carbohydrates that are slowly metabolized by the body, they are also full of vitamins and minerals, most notably iron. When boiled without peeling they give off a sticky black sap that is difficult to wash off the saucepan, so it is best to peel them first.

16–20 green bananas
Pickle:
1lb/500g small cucumbers, peeled and very finely chopped
1/4 cup/1 medium onion, finely chopped
Salt to taste
1/2 cup/5 tablespoons parsley, finely chopped

Fresh hot pepper very finely chopped, to taste
1 medium sweet pepper, finely chopped
3-6 tablespoons lime juice, to taste

Garnish: Parsley and sweet pepper rings

1. Oil hands before peeling green bananas to avoid getting hands stained with sap. The sap from green bananas stains clothes and is very hard to remove. Peel the green bananas. Cut a slit down the length of the banana skin, cut off either end of the banana and attempt to split the skin open and pull it off. If this fails, simply peel the banana with a knife. Boil in salted water immediately to avoid discolouration, until tender.
2. Meanwhile, prepare the pickle ingredients and mix well. Remove any seeds from the cucumber. Put enough salt and lime juice to give the pickle a good twang, since the green bananas soak it up quickly.
3. Place bananas in pickle in a bowl and refrigerate. Should be served within 2 or 3 hours.
4. Place in a serving dish and garnish with parsley and sweet pepper rings.

barbecued fish

One of the secrets to the successful preparation of barbecued fish is to use an oil-based marinade. Remember, too, that fish needs very little time over the heat in order to be cooked through. One final tip to delicious barbecued fish: it is much tastier when placed directly over the heat in a folding fish rack, wrapping in foil tends to steam the fish.

6 servings of fish fillets (3-4lbs/1.5-2kg)
suggested varieties include tuna,
dorado/mahi mahi, salmon, barracuda,
snapper, wahoo or marlin
2 tablespoons of Caribbean seasoning

2 cloves fresh garlic finely chopped
1/2 cup 4floz/125ml olive oil
1 lime
1 tablespoon salt
3 cups 24floz/750ml water

1. Marinate the fillets of fish in the lime, salt and water for about 10 minutes.
2. Rinse and drain fish.
3. Mix seasoning, garlic and oil in a shallow dish and place fish in marinade, coating well. Marinate at room temperature for at least 1/2 hour or overnight in the fridge.
4. If possible, remove from the fridge a couple of hours before cooking.
5. Place the fish on the grill in a folding fish rack if you have one. Barbecue over a high heat for 2-4 minutes on each side, depending on the type of fish and how rare you prefer it.

Serve immediately.

Serves 6

fish in white sauce

This dish can be made ahead of time, stored in the fridge and baked just before serving. It is especially delicious when served with boiled or mashed potatoes and vegetables, such as carrots, pumpkin or string beans with almonds. It may be enhanced by including seafood such as shrimp and lobster. To transform this fish into a one pot meal, add cooked yam or potatoes diced, grated cheese and chopped tomatoes.

4 servings of fish fillets such as dorado, wahoo, salmon or any firm fish
2 cups 16floz/500ml water
1 teaspoon dried mixed herbs or a tablespoon fresh thyme, parsley and marjoram finely chopped
1 tablespoon onion powder or grated onion
1 teaspoon garlic powder or one clove garlic finely chopped
1/2 stock cube, chicken or fish
1/2 teaspoon of salt

White pepper to taste
2 tablespoons margarine or butter
1/4 cup/4 tablespoons flour
2 cups 16floz/500ml milk
1 tablespoon parmesan cheese
1/4 cup/4 tablespoons dry white wine (optional)
3 hard-boiled eggs, shelled (optional)

Garnish: Fine breadcrumbs and parmesan cheese

1. Place the fish fillets in a saucepan with water, garlic, onion powder, salt, white pepper, herbs and the 1/2 stock cube. Bring to the boil and simmer for 3-5 minutes or until cooked (Fish needs very little cooking and if overcooked can be tough).
2. Remove the fish from the stock and set aside. Reserve the stock in a jug.
3. Over a medium to high heat melt the butter or margarine and add the flour to make a fairly dry roux. Gradually add the milk. Remove from the heat each time the milk comes to the boil, beating with a wooden spoon to blend. Add 2 cups of the fish stock, the herbs, the wine and parmesan cheese. Simmer over a medium to high heat, stirring until the sauce thickens.

4. Option 1

Remove from the heat, break the fish into chunks and add to the sauce. Preheat a moderate oven 350F, 180C or Gas Mark 4. Grease a casserole dish, slice and arrange the hard boiled eggs in the bottom and pour the fish mixture over. Top with a little butter and some fine breadcrumbs or parmesan cheese. Bake for 20 minutes.

Option 2

Pipe four portions of hot mashed potatoes. Heat the 4 servings of poached fish and place on top of the mashed potatoes. Pour over the sauce. Place the vegetables on the plate and serve immediately.

Serves 4

stewed down salt fish

Salt fish and cou cou is the national dish of Barbados. Salt fish was imported from Canada as a cheap source of protein for the slaves and this dish represents the culinary ingenuity of Barbadians.

1lb boneless salted cod
2oz/60g butter
2 medium onions, thinly sliced
2 tablespoons finely chopped garlic
1 sweet pepper thinly sliced
2 cups 16oz/500ml tinned tomatoes or 2lbs/1kg peeled fresh tomatoes, sliced
1 tablespoon curry powder

1 sprig fresh thyme
1 sprig fresh marjoram
2 sprigs fresh parsley, finely chopped
1/2 cup 20floz/600ml water
Salt and freshly ground pepper to taste
1 teaspoon pepper sauce
4 hard-boiled eggs (optional)

1. Boil salt fish in plenty of water for 20 minutes. If still too salty, repeat. Drain salt fish, break into wedges, check for bones and set aside.
2. Heat butter and sauté the onion. When beginning to brown, add garlic, salt fish and sweet pepper and sauté for a further 3 minutes.
3. Add tomatoes, curry powder, herbs, water, pepper sauce and black pepper and simmer uncovered for 15 minutes to an hour or until tender. Salt to taste.
4. If adding eggs, shell and slice them and add to the salt fish about 10 minutes before it's finished cooking.

Serves 4

cou cou

This cou cou recipe is different in that the corn meal is blended with cold water ahead of cooking it with the okras. This makes it smooth and much quicker to prepare.

2 1/2 cups 12oz corn meal
1–2 teaspoons salt
Water
8oz/250g okras
2 tablespoons chopped onion
2oz/60g butter

1. Process the corn meal and 1 teaspoon salt with 3 cups of water in a blender.
2. Cut the tops off the okras, wash and slice thinly into circles. Place okras in a medium saucepan with 3 cups of water, and chopped onion. Bring to the boil and simmer for 10 minutes. Strain into a heat proof jug and place the okras back into the saucepan along with the butter and blended corn meal.
3. Place the saucepan with the corn meal over a medium heat and very gradually add the okra water, stirring to blend.
4. Once all okra water is added, lower the heat, cover and steam.

Serves 4

fried fish or chicken bajan style

Bajan offerings of fried fish and chicken are almost always exceptionally delicious. Three reasons for this are: the fish and chicken are soaked in lime, salt, and water during preparation; they are then marinated or stuffed with savoury Bajan seasonings; and they are fried in soft, home-seasoned breadcrumbs.

Fish fillets or chicken parts to serve 4
2 limes (use one if they are large and juicy)
2 teaspoons salt
2 tablespoons Bajan seasoning
1 egg
1 cup 5oz/155g extra fine breadcrumbs
1 cup 5oz/155g flour
Salt and white pepper to taste
1 teaspoon paprika
1 teaspoon chicken or fish multi purpose seasoning (optional)
Oil for frying (Canola or Olive are reputedly healthier)

Salt Breads

Fried fish is often sold sandwiched in a soft but chewy white bread bun and referred to as a fish cutter.

1. Squeeze the limes into a bowl with 3/4 cup of water, add the salt and place the fish or chicken to soak for about 1/2 hour. Remove the fish or chicken, rinse and pat dry.

2. Whisk the egg in a medium bowl with some salt and white pepper and if you are doing fish, the seasoning. Put the fish into the egg and seasoning mixture. If you are doing chicken, make a couple of incisions in each piece, insert some seasoning and place in the egg. It is best if the fish or chicken is allowed to sit in the egg for an hour or so to allow the flavours to permeate.

3. Mix the flour, breadcrumbs, white pepper, paprika and a little salt. This is one of those occasions when you can add various seasonings out of your kitchen cupboard like fish and chicken magic, onion and garlic powder, dried herbs or whatever takes your fancy.

4. Heat very shallow oil for fish and slightly deeper for chicken, in a large frying pan over a medium/high heat. Shake off excess egg, coat in the breadcrumb mixture, shake again and place in the oil when it is hot enough (It should sizzle slightly when the item is placed in it). Fry the fish over the medium/high heat for a couple of minutes on each side. Fish needs very little cooking and is overcooked very easily. If frying flying fish place it skin side up first. Fry chicken over a medium/low heat to allow it to cook through without burning or getting too dark (10-15 minutes on each side depending on how large the piece of chicken is).

5. Drain on absorbent paper and place on a warm dish.

Serves 4

big soup

This is a very filling and healthy soup. It is fat-free, easy to digest and full of nutrients. Lamb, crab or fish can be used instead of chicken. A wide variety of other vegetables can be included such as green bananas, yams, okras, eddoes, breadfruit, mushrooms, corn, leeks, squash and zucchini to name a few. Add the slower cooking vegetables such as yams and green bananas first and the faster cooking vegetables such as mushrooms, okras and zucchini for a few minutes just before the soup is finished cooking.

1lb/500g chicken parts with skin and bones

Stock:
9 cups 45floz/1.35l of water
1–2 large sprigs of thyme, parsley and marjoram
Celery leaves or a stick of celery
1–2 whole, green topped spring onions
Ground black pepper to taste
1 onion
2 cloves garlic
1 chicken stock cube
Vegetables

3 medium English potatoes, cut in chunks
1 medium sweet potato, cut in chunks
3 carrots cut in 1" pieces
1 small onion, finely chopped
A sprig of thyme and marjoram whole
2 spring onions (scallions) whole
1lb/500g pumpkin, cut in chunks
1 stick celery, chopped
1 medium sweet pepper, cubed
2 cups 10oz/315g cauliflower, broken into florets
2 cups 10oz/315g broccoli florets

1. Wash the chicken parts and remove any excess fat. Do not remove the skin yet since it gives the stock a good flavour. Place the chicken and all the stock ingredients in a large saucepan. Once brought to the boil, reduce heat to medium and simmer for about 1/2 hour.

2. Remove chicken and strain the stock. It should yield about eight cups stock.
3. Put the stock, onion, fresh herbs, spring onions, English and sweet potatoes and carrots into the saucepan, bring to the boil and then simmer for about 10 minutes.
4. Cut up the chicken into bite size pieces.
5. Add the pumpkin, celery, sweet pepper, cauliflower, chicken and broccoli and continue to simmer for another 5 or 10 minutes until the vegetables are cooked.
6. Remove the spring onions and sprigs of herbs before serving. Add salt and pepper to taste.

Serves 4 as a main course and 8 as an appetizer.

pudding and souse

Pudding, made with sweet potato, is generally stuffed into pig's intestine and steamed as black or white pudding, but is quite nice steamed in a pudding bowl. It is served with souse (following page).

Pudding:
2-3 lbs/1-1.5kg sweet potato
2-3 green topped spring onions, finely chopped
2 tablespoons fresh thyme leaves
2 tablespoons fresh marjoram

4 tablespoons butter
1 tablespoon light brown sugar
1/2 teaspoon powdered cloves
1 very hot bonnet or chilli pepper
1-2 tablespoons flour (optional)

1. Peel and grate the sweet potato on the very fine, but bumpy side of the grater that gives the finest texture.
2. Mix the grated sweet potato with the herbs, butter, sugar, cloves and minced hot pepper. Add enough hot water to make a soft but not runny texture. Add 1 or 2 tablespoons flour if the sweet potatoes are not very starchy and the mixture is too runny.
3. Pour into a pyrex or metal steaming bowl and steam over boiling water for an hour or until an inserted scewer comes out clean.

Steeped in tradition, souse in Barbados is usually made with pig's head and trotters.
However pork chops, with the skin on, are easier to find and cook and make an excellent,
less fatty, very tasty souse. Conch also makes a delicious souse. Pudding and souse is
made and sold throughout Barbados every Saturday. Although generally eaten as a main
course dish with pudding and pickled breadfruit, soused pork chops make an excellent
canapé or appetizer.

Souse:
1/2 pig's head
3 cups 24floz/725ml water
1 onion
Bunch of herbs
Pepper sauce, black pepper and salt to taste
1 chicken stock cube (optional)
2 cups/3-6 peeled cucumbers, finely chopped – choose cucumbers with as few seeds as possible

1/2 cup/2 medium onions, finely chopped
1/3 cup lime juice (juice of 2 or 3 limes, enough to give the pickle a good twang)
1 teaspoon salt
Small bunch parsley, finely chopped
1 teaspoon hot pepper, very finely chopped or 1/2 teaspoon red pepper sauce – adjust to taste

To garnish:
Sweet pepper rings and parsley

1. Wash and clean the pig's head and place in a saucepan with water, onion, herbs, pepper sauce, pepper, salt and stock cube if using. It is said, "de sweeter de souse water, de sweeter de souse". Bring to the boil and simmer for about 1/2 hour or until the pork is tender.
2. Meanwhile, prepare the pickle of cucumber, onion, lime juice, salt, parsley and hot pepper and refrigerate.
3. When pig's head is cooked, strain off the liquid, reserving a little and allow to cool. Remove meat from the bone and cut into strips crossways (each slice should have skin, fat and meat and be about 1" thick).
4. Add the sliced pork to the pickle and mix well. Souse should be eaten within 6 or 8 hours of being made, as the pickle tends to deteriorate after that.
5. Serve garnished with parsley and sweet pepper rings.

bajan stewed down chops

This is hearty fare for lunch or dinner that is popular with all ages. Delicious served with mashed potatoes or rice and steamed vegetables.

4 servings of pork chops (preferably with the skin on) or lamb chops
2 tablespoons olive oil
8 medium onions, quartered and sliced
1 cup/2 sweet peppers, diced
2 tablespoons garlic, finely chopped
1 teaspoon grated nutmeg
2 tablespoons fresh thyme or

1 tablespoon dried thyme
Pepper sauce to taste
A few dashes of worcestershire sauce
A few dashes of Angostura bitters
2 cups 14floz/425ml can peeled tomatoes, diced
2 cups 16floz/500ml water

1. Rub salt on to the pork chops and leave for 10 minutes. Wash and pat dry.
2. Heat the oil in a large frying pan and brown the chops on both sides over a medium to high heat (about 10 mins). Remove the chops from the pan and set aside.
3. Sauté the onions until beginning to brown, add the garlic and sweet peppers and sauté for a further couple of minutes. Add the tomatoes, nutmeg, thyme, worcestershire sauce, Angostura bitters, water and replace the pork chops.
4. Cover and simmer over a low heat until the chops are tender (1-2 hours). Add more water during cooking if necessary.

Serves 4

roast pork

Roast Pork is especially delicious in Barbados. Pigs played an important sociological role in the island, reared and slaughtered in back yards, they supplemented the meagre wages of the workers and saw many a family through hard times or financed their betterment. The revered leg and shoulder roasts are the prized parts of the pig. Incisions are made into the pork and filled with Bajan Seasoning. The skin is scored into tiny squares and you can usually rely on it becoming delicious, crispy crackling.

Bajan seasoning (page 6)
Limes
Salt
Yellow American mustard
Water

Gravy
2 tablespoons pork fat or olive oil, if you prefer
2 tablespoons flour (Use more if you like a thick gravy and less if you like a thin gravy)
3 cups liquid from the roasting tin
Worcestershire sauce to taste
Salt and freshly ground black pepper
1 tablespoon onion powder
1 teaspoon gravy browning

Tip
Scoring the skin of the pork when it is still partially frozen is a little easier than scoring after it has defrosted.

1. Rub the fresh or frozen pork in plenty of salt, place in plastic bag and put in the bottom of the fridge overnight or for up to 2 days. Wash the pork, pat dry and coat in lime juice and salt.
2. Using a long sharp knife, make deep incisions strategically in the joint and push in Bajan seasoning. Score the skin into 1" squares. Lather each piece of skin with plenty of yellow American mustard. The mustard and its flavour completely disappears and gives delicious crispy crackling.
3. Place in an open roasting pan with 2" of water. Pork is suitable for either fast or slow roasting. A larger joint is better cooked in a slower oven so that the outside doesn't overcook before the center is well done. Pork should always be eaten well cooked, rare pork can contain harmful bacteria that may cause severe illness.
In order to have a delicious gravy

stock, keep the liquid topped up in the roasting pan during cooking. Do not cover during roasting.

Fast Roasting - Small to medium roasts.
25 minutes per lb/500g, 25 minutes over.
Preheat the oven to hot 450F, 220C or Gas Mark 6. After 20 minutes of cooking, lower to moderately hot, 400F, 200C or Gas Mark 5.
Slow Roasting - Medium to large roasts.
35 minutes per lb/500g, 35 minutes over.

Preheat oven at moderate 350F, 180C or Gas Mark 4 and keep at this setting.

The pork is well cooked when it is skewered right to the center of the roast and only a minimal amount of clear liquid comes out. Remove the roast from the pan and set aside to cool. Pour the dripping and liquid out of the roasting pan into a jug. (Separator jug if possible).

glazed ham with hot sorrel sauce

This traditional Christmas fare is ideal for a buffet at any time of the year. It can also be made with a small picnic ham and served as a family treat, carving the hot ham at the table. The earthy and tangy taste of sorrel goes perfectly with ham, but if this juice is unavailable, supplement with cider or pineapple juice. Fresh sorrel is only sold around Christmas but dried sorrel is available throughout the year so you can make the sorrel drink by simply steeping the dried sepals in boiling water with some cloves, cinnamon and fresh ginger and adding sugar to taste.

1 pre-cooked ham approx. 8lb /4kg
2 1/2 cups 20floz/600ml sorrel drink
1/2 cup 6oz/185g light brown sugar
1 teaspoon ground cloves
1 teaspoon ground cinnamon

The rind and juice of 1 lime
1 cup 5oz/155g raisins/sultanas
3 teaspoons English hot dry mustard
2 tablespoons corn starch or arrowroot
2 tablespoons cold water

1. Remove most of the fat from the ham, leaving a thin layer to seal the ham. Place ham, fat side up in a roasting pan.
2. Combine sorrel, half of the brown sugar (1/4 cup), powdered clove and cinnamon, 2 teaspoons English hot dry mustard (the third teaspoon is for the ham glaze) and lime rind and juice and pour over the ham.
3. Cover with baking tin lid or foil and bake the ham at 325F, 160C or Gas Mark 3, basting frequently, for 1 1/2 hours.
4. Add raisins to the pan and bake for 1/2 hour longer.
5. Remove the ham from the oven and pour off the pan liquid with raisins. Combine remaining 1/4 cup of the brown sugar with remaining teaspoon dry mustard and press onto ham. Half hour before you are going to eat, bake the ham uncovered for about 30 minutes longer in a hotter oven 400F, 200C or Gas Mark 5, to set the glaze.

6. To make the hot sorrel sauce skim off the fat from the pan juices. This can be done quickly using a fat separator or simply by spooning off the top. Mix the corn starch or arrowroot flour with 2 tablespoons water. Place the pan juices including the raisins into a medium saucepan, add in the corn starch mixture, bring to the boil and then reduce the heat to simmer, stirring constantly until it is thickened. Set aside to reheat when ready to serve.

7. After the ham has baked with the glaze, heat the sorrel sauce and pour a small amount over the ham. Serve the rest in a gravy boat.

pepperpot

This method of cooking and preserving meat was introduced by the indigenous Amerindian population of Guyana and it has become a traditional dish served in Barbadian homes at Christmas and on family vacations when there are lots of hungry mouths at every meal time. Cassareep is a thick, black preservative sauce made from Cassava, a root crop. This hot, spicy, slightly sweet, almost black stew is delicious served with mashed sweet potato or steamed rice. The traditional businessmen's clubs in the Caribbean islands' capitals such as Bridgetown and Georgetown were said to have had the same pepperpot on the go for years, continuously adding ingredients and boiling it up daily.

3lbs/1.5kg beef oxtails with skin if poss.
2lbs/1kg fresh pig feet
1lb/1/2kg cow heel
1.5lb/750g salted pork or beef
3-4lbs/750-1000g chicken
4lb/2kg beef stew
3 onions
Large bouquet garni of fresh thyme and marjoram
4-6 scotch bonnet or chilli peppers (As hot as possible)
2 cups 16floz/500ml cassareep

Pepperpot Rules

1. Vegetables or starchy foods should not be added to pepperpot. This pepperpot should not be confused with the thick vegetable pepperpot soup served in the northern Caribbean.
2. Lamb should never be added to pepperpot.
3. If not frozen, pepperpot must be kept covered and boiled up everyday for 1/2 hour, if kept out of the fridge.

1. Cut up and brown the beef oxtails, cow heel, pig feet and salted beef or pork, place in water and simmer for 1-2 hours or pressure cook for 45 minutes.
2. Cut up the chicken and beef and onions and fry in a little oil. Add water and bouquet garni and simmer until tender but firm.

3. Place the two stews in a large stainless steel pot, remove the bouquet garni and add the cassareep while meat is still hot. Tie up the peppers in a small muslin bag and place in the saucepan. You can use a square of thin cloth and a piece of string. Simmer on a low heat until the pepperpot thickens. (About 4 hours).

4. Hot water and cassareep may be added when more sauce is needed, and more meat can be fried and added. Pepperpot can be kept without refrigeration, but it must be boiled up everyday for 1/2 hour or more and kept covered. If the pepperpot is not being eaten on a daily basis it is best to freeze the pepperpot after the initial serving. The daily boiling which is required, overcooks the meats making them hard and very stringy.

Serves 20-25

bajan beef stew

Barbados is famous for tasty stews and their secret is the pungent combination of pepper sauce and fresh herbs. Beetroots, carrots and the delicious nutty taste of green bananas lighten up the traditionally spicy Bajan beef stew but the recipe is still delicious without them. Green bananas are loaded with vitamins and minerals, most notably iron. Serve with rice.

1 tablespoon vegetable oil
1 1/2 lbs/750g stew beef
1 medium onion
2 tablespoons garlic, finely chopped
2 tablespoons Bajan seasoning (optional)
6 cups 48floz/1.5l water
1/2 tablespoon gravy browning
1/2 teaspoon pepper sauce
1/2 stick celery
1 sprig fresh thyme (1/2 teaspoon dried)

1 sprig fresh marjoram (1/2 teaspoon dried)
1 beef stock cube
1 tablespoon butter (optional)
3 tablespoons flour (optional)
1 bay leaf
1/2lb/250g carrots
1 large/2 small beetroot
Salt and freshly ground pepper to taste
1lb/500g green bananas peeled (optional)

1. Wash beef, pat dry and cut into very small cubes. Place in a bowl with the onion, garlic, pepper sauce, seasoning (optional),celery, herbs and beef cube. Mix well and leave to marinate if possible.
2. Heat the oil and sauté beef for a few minutes, add water and the gravy browning and bring to the boil. Reduce heat to medium and simmer until tender (40 minutes to an hour depending on the quality of the beef).
3. Mix butter and flour into a paste and add to the stew to thicken, stirring until well blended. Add salt and pepper, bayleaf, carrots, beetroot and green bananas (if including) and simmer until the vegetables are tender (about 15 mins).

Serves 4-6

bajan patties

Hot and spicy meat filled patties are sold in glass cabinets throughout Barbados. The recipe below contains potato, which helps to thicken the filling. However, if you prefer to leave this ingredient out, then thicken with flour. Other vegetables may also be added to make a more nutritious, light meal. Note that the filling needs to be cold when making the patties, so it has to be made ahead of time and refrigerated. Smaller versions are popular at cocktail parties.

Filling
2 tablespoons oil
1 cup/3 medium onions, finely chopped
1 tablespoon garlic, finely chopped
12oz/360g minced beef
12floz/360ml medium tin peeled
tomatoes (or 1 cup 8floz/250ml chunky
pasta sauce)
1 beef stock cube
1 teaspoon dried thyme or 1 tablespoon
fresh thyme leaves
1/4 cup/2-3 chopped green topped spring
onions/scallions
Freshly ground peppercorns and salt
1 cup 8floz/250ml water
A few dashes of worcestershire sauce
Red or yellow pepper sauce or fresh hot
pepper to taste
2 cups/4 medium diced raw potato

Pastry
5oz/155g lard
5oz/155g margarine
3 cups 1lb/500g flour
1 teaspoon salt
1 tablespoon curry powder or English
hot mustard powder
1/4-1 cup 8floz/250ml very cold water
Different flours require very different
amounts of water. In the Caribbean the
flour tends to require the full cup. The
golden rule is simply put enough water
to make the pastry hold together well. A
pastry with dry cracks is difficult to role
out.
1 egg for brushing the patties

Makes 20-24 patties

Filling

1. The filling for these patties has to be cold, so it needs to be made ahead of time and refrigerated.
2. Heat the oil in a medium saucepan, and sauté the onions. As they begin to soften and brown slightly add the garlic, scallions and minced beef. Continue to sauté for a few minutes.
3. Cut up the tinned tomatoes and add to the beef along with the crumbled beef stock cube, thyme, worcestershire sauce, pepper sauce to taste, water, potatoes, black pepper and salt to taste.
4. Simmer over a low to medium heat until the liquid is almost all evaporated.
5. Cool and refrigerate.

Pastry

1. To make pastry in a food processor, the lard and margarine should be very cold. This can be a challenge in the warm Caribbean. Either store them in your freezer and shred them into the flour or if they are in the fridge, cut them up into fingernail size pieces and harden in the freezer for 10 minutes.
2. Sieve the flour, salt and curry powder or mustard into a food processor. Add the margarine and lard. Process for 30 seconds. Do not over process.
3. Tip into a bowl, pour in the very cold water and mix with a flat knife.
4. Knead gently with the tips of your fingers, just enough to form a ball. Wrap in waxed paper and refrigerate for 1/2 hour.

Patties

1. Preheat the oven at 375F, 190C or Gas Mark 4.
2. Roll out the pastry. Cut in circles 3-4" in diameter. Place the meat in the centre. Wet the edge of the circle with water and fold over to form a crescent. Press down with a fork or your fingers to seal the patty. Cut or stick a little hole in the top of the patty to let the steam out when it is baking.
3. Place on a well greased baking sheet and brush with beaten egg. Bake for 25-30 minutes.
4. If you are preparing them well before serving or freezing them, you can cook them for 15-20 minutes and finish baking them just before serving.

sticky pineapple upside down cake

The pineapple was another fruit that was introduced to the world from the Caribbean, not being taken to Hawaii until the mid 1800's.

To line the tin
1/2 cup 4oz/125g sugar
2oz/60g butter
1/4 cup 2floz/60ml golden sugar
1/4 cup water
1 large tin 20oz/567g sliced pineapple
1 lime (optional)
10-15 glacé or maraschino cherries
A few sticks of angelica (optional)

Cake
6oz/185g butter or margarine
3/4 cup 6oz/185g sugar
2 teaspoons vanilla essence
3 eggs
1/2 cup reserved juice from the tin
1 cup 6oz/185g flour
3 teaspoons baking powder (if using self-raising flour only use one teaspoon baking powder)
1/2 teaspoon salt

1. To make the caramel, place the water, sugar, butter and golden syrup in a saucepan. Bring to the boil and simmer for 5-10mins.
2. Pour half the caramel into the pan and reserve the other half to heat up and pour over just before serving. Put the pineapple slices on top of the caramel in the pan and squeeze a little lime juice on them. This gives a little welcome tartness to the pineapple that contrasts well with the sweet caramel. Reserve the juice from the tin to put in the cake mixture. Decorate with the cherries (and angelica). Set aside.
3. Preheat a moderate oven 325F, 160C or Gas Mark 3.
4. Place all the cake ingredients into a food processor in the order they are listed, sifting the flour, baking powder and salt.
5. Process for 20-25 seconds (no longer). Drop in spoonfuls on top of the pineapples in the pan and spread the mixture carefully. Bake in the centre of the oven for 30-35 minutes or until the cake is golden brown, firm to the touch and an inserted skewer comes out clean.
6. Turn out on to a platter, pour heated reserved caramel over the top and serve hot or at room temperature.

Serves 8-10

chocolate icebox pudding

1 store bought sponge cake (made without butter or shortening, if possible)
1/4 cup/4 tablespoons cream sherry
8oz/250g semi-sweet chocolate (bar or chocolate chips)
4 eggs

4 tablespoons whipping cream
4 tablespoons sugar
Garnish: 1 cup whipping cream and 1 small square of chocolate (reserved from the bar) or semi sweet chocolate chips

1. Slice up the sponge cake and divide in half. Put the first half in the bottom of a 10" dessert dish. Sprinkle with 1/8 cup of sherry. Set aside the rest of the sponge and sherry.
2. Melt chocolate in a double boiler, or in a covered bowl on a saucepan of boiling water, reserving a small square or a few chocolate chips for garnishing.
3. Separate the eggs, being extremely careful not to get any yolk in the whites. It is best to separate each egg into a little bowl, so that if you make a slip it doesn't affect all the egg whites. Place the egg whites into a very dry, clean, medium mixing bowl.
4. Place the yolks in a small mixing bowl along with the sugar and beat with an electric beater until creamy.
5. Take the melted chocolate off the heat and add the beaten egg yolk mixture and 4 tablespoons of cream.
6. Wash and dry the beater blades thoroughly. Beat the egg whites until as light and fluffy as possible, (about 5 minutes).
7. Fold the beaten egg whites into the chocolate mixture until well blended.
8. Scoop half of this on to the sherry soaked cake in the dish. Place the rest of the cake slices, sprinkle with sherry and top with the rest of the chocolate mixture.
9. Cover and refrigerate. A short while before serving, whisk the double cream until stiff and place on top of the pudding. The cream will whip most successfully if you chill the bowl with the cream in the freezer for about 10 minutes just before whisking. Sprinkle on the reserved chocolate chips or grate the reserved chocolate on top, using the large side of the grater.

Serves 8

baked custard

There are many variations to this custard. It can be an exotic ginger custard by adding a teaspoon of fresh grated ginger to the custard and then garnished with ground ginger when baked. The water can be replaced with a can of unsweetened creme of coconut to make a delicious coconut creme custard. Add a teaspoon of finely grated orange peel and replace the water with orange juice for an orange creme custard. Guava stew can be placed in the bottom of the dish before pouring in the custard and baking.

1 tin 8floz/250ml condensed milk
1 tin 8floz/250ml water
4 eggs
1 teaspoon vanilla essence
1 tablespoon butter

Garnish: Freshly grated nutmeg

1. Preheat the oven to 325F, 160C or Gas Mark 4
2. Place the condensed milk, water, eggs, vanilla essence and butter in a blender and blend for a minute.
3. Pour into a 8"/20cm diameter dish that is about 2"/5cm deep. Garnish with grated nutmeg.
4. Place in a pan of boiling water and place carefully in the oven. Bake for 35-40 minutes. It is ready when an inserted skewer comes out clean.

Serves 4-6

chocolate fudge

This is a delicate recipe that must be followed to the letter in order to be successful. If you don't boil it long enough, or if you beat it too little, the fudge won't set. On the other hand, if you boil it too long, or beat it too much, it's likely to set in the saucepan or become too hot and thus set in unattractive crystalized lumps.

2 1/2 cups 1lb/500g light brown sugar
1/2 cup 4floz/125ml milk
6oz/185g butter
1 cup 3oz/90g cocoa

3 teaspoons vanilla essence

6"x10"/15cmx25cm pan buttered

1. Put the sugar and milk in a medium pan and bring to the boil.
2. Add the cocoa and butter and stir over a medium/high heat until the butter has completely melted and the cocoa is blended in.
3. Reduce the heat to low and simmer without stirring, for 5-8 minutes. It is ready to beat when a drop of the mixture forms a soft ball in a saucer of cool water.
4. Remove from the heat and add the vanilla essence. Then tilt the pan and beat vigorously for about three minutes until the fudge gets quite thick but still pourable. Be careful not to beat the fudge for too long as it may set right there in the saucepan, if you beat it too little, however, it won't set at all and you'll end up with chocolate toffee. Also, be very careful not to splatter this mixture or spill it on yourself or anyone else - hot fudge can give a serious burn.
5. Pour into the buttered pan.
6. As it begins to set, (about 10 minutes) score with pointed knife into 1" squares. Completely sets in about 20 minutes.
7. Once set, turn it out with one firm knock upside down on to a wooden chopping board. Break into individual pieces along the score lines.
8. Store in an airtight container or package in wax paper.

coconut bread/banana bread

Coconut Bread: *This is a sweet, stodgy bread that goes well with an early morning mug or afternoon cup of tea. This recipe, prepared to yield two moist coconut breads, may be adjusted by halving the margarine to create a dryer loaf.*

Banana Bread: *This nutritious Caribbean speciality is a great way to use up over-ripe bananas. It is deliciously moist so there is no temptation to spread it with butter.*

Coconut Bread

12oz/375g margarine or butter
2 tsp vanilla essence
1 cup 8oz/250g brown sugar
2 eggs
1/2 cup 4 floz/120ml water or coconut water
8oz/250g grated coconut
2 2/3 cups 16oz/500g flour

Dash cinnamon, mixed spice, nutmeg
2 teaspoons baking powder (heaping)
1/2 cup/6 tablespoons raisins (optional)
1/2 cup glacé cherries (optional)

Garnish: Light brown sugar, grated
coconut and cherries

1. Preheat oven to 325F, 160C or Gas Mark 3. Grease two small loaf tins. Cut two rips of paper the length of the tins and the height of the two sides plus two inches. Place along the tin with an inch protruding at each end, which you use to easily lift the cooked bread out of the tin.
2. Place all the ingredients in a food processor in the order they are listed, sifting in the flour and reserving 4 tbsps of coconut. Process for 20 seconds.
3. Add the raisins if you are including these and process for a further 5 seconds.
4. Place the mixture in the two loaf tins in equal amounts. Make a ditch down the centre of the bread and fill with most of the reserved coconut, covering it with the mixture so that it is in the middle of the finished bread. This can be spiced up with a pinch of cinnamon and nutmeg and a little sugar to taste. Sprinkle the top with sugar, the rest of the reserved grated coconut and cherries, if using.
6. Bake in the centre of the oven for about an hour or until an inserted skewer comes out clean. Lift out onto racks and cool.

Banana Bread

1 1/2 cups 7oz/220g whole-wheat flour
1 tsp baking soda
1 tsp baking powder
1/2 tsp salt
1/3 cup 3floz/100ml oil
2/3 cup 6oz/185g brown sugar
2 eggs

6 medium bananas (very ripe is best)
2 tbsps molasses (optional)
Raisins & chopped nuts (optional)
1 tsp cinnamon
1 tsp nutmeg
1 tsp clove
1 tsp vanilla essence

1. Preheat oven to 350F, 180C or Gas Mark 3. Grease two medium loaf tins. Cut two strips of paper the length of the tins plus the height of the two ends plus two inches. Place along the tin with an inch protruding at each end, which you use to easily lift the cooked bread out of the tin.
2. Place all the ingredients in a food processor and process for 20 seconds (Do not over process). Finally, add raisins and chopped nuts, if desired and process for a further 5 seconds.
3. Place in the two loaf tins. Sprinkle with extra cinnamon and sugar.
4. Bake for 50 minutes or until an inserted skewer comes out clean. Lift out onto racks and allow to cool.

ginger bread

This delicious old fashioned recipe uses the very easy melting method.

1/2 cup 3oz/90g sugar
2oz/60g butter
2oz/60g lard
1/2 cup 4floz/125ml golden syrup
1/2 cup 4floz/125ml molasses/treacle (use a full cup of golden syrup, if you're not using molasses/treacle)
1/4 cup water

1/2 teaspoon ground clove
1/2 teaspoon salt
1 teaspoon ground cinnamon
1/4 cup/4 tablespoons ground ginger
2 1/2 cups 14oz/440g flour
1 egg
1 1/2 teaspoons baking soda

1. Preheat the oven to 325F, 160C or Gas Mark 3.
2. Grease a 10"/25cm square pan or equivalent. Cut a piece of wax paper the sum width of the bottom and two sides of the tin plus 2"/5cm. Line the tin with wax paper sticking up at either side, which will be used to easily lift the cooked bread out of the tin. Grease this and dust the pan with a little flour.
3. Melt the butter, lard, syrup, water and sugar in a medium saucepan.
4. Sift the dry ingredients into a medium mixing bowl.
5. Whisk an egg and add to the dry ingredients along with the melted ingredients and mix well.
6. Bake for about 45 minutes or until a skewer comes out clean.
7. Turn out and cool on a wire rack.
8. Cut into squares.

marble cake

This is a good cake for children's parties or just to make with children for the fun of it. The icing is especially funky and quite easy to do. You can let your creativity flow and decorate with little coloured sweets or candy such as smarties, fruit jellies and wine gums. Another possibility is to bake it in two small loaf tins and make an enchanted house, cutting the second loaf into the shape of a roof and covering it with candies. The orange rind and juice in the icing gives the whole cake a subtle orange flavour.

6oz/185g softened butter or margarine
3/4 cup 6oz/185g granulated sugar
3 eggs
1/2 cup 4floz/125ml milk
1 teaspoon vanilla essence
1 cup 6oz/185g flour
3 heaping teaspoons baking powder (if
using self raising flour reduce baking
powder to 1 teaspoon)
1/2 teaspoon salt
Red, blue, yellow and green food dye

Icing
2 cups 12oz/375g icing sugar
2-3 tablespoons freshly squeezed
orange juice
1 teaspoon finely grated orange rind
Red, blue, yellow and green food dye
Garnish: sprinkles, jellies, smarties
etc.

1. Preheat a moderate oven 350F,180C or Gas Mark 4.
2. Grease two 7"/18cm or 8"/20cm cake tins, cut out a circle of greaseproof paper and line each tin, butter the surface of the paper and dust with flour.
3. Place all ingredients except the food dyes, in the order that they are listed into a food processor, sifting in the flour, baking powder and salt. (Break each egg into a small bowl before putting into the processor to varify their freshness). Process for 20 seconds (Do not over process).

4. To dye the cake mix into four different colours, place three quarters of the cake mix in three small bowls leaving the fourth quarter of cake mix in the processor. Squirt a couple of drops of each colour food dye into each bowl and the food processor and mix in, stirring as little as possible. You can mix the one in the food processor by processing for a second. Place 1/2 of each colour in each baking pan and spread.

5. Bake in the centre of the oven for approx. 20 minutes until risen, golden brown and a skewer inserted into the centre comes out clean.

6. Turn out the cakes onto a wire rack to cool, removing the paper backing.

7. Sift the icing sugar, add the orange rind and gradually add the orange juice to make a spreading consistency.

8. Divide the icing into four separate little bowls. You can leave a quarter in the original bowl and squirt two drops of each colour dye into each bowl and mix well.

9. Place one cake on a cake plate, place 1/2 of each colour icing strategically on each quarter of the cake. Spread the icing in a circular motion in the same direction so that each colour runs into the next. Repeat on the top and decorate. This recipe gives enough icing to ice the sides of the cake so if you prefer to ice only the top and middle (for simplicity) you can use 8oz icing sugar and 1 1/2 tablespoons of orange juice.

index